FIGHTER AIRCRAFT

Published in 2009 by Sandcastle Books Ltd

Orchard House,
6, Butt Furlong
Fladbury
Worcestershire, UK
WR10 2QZ

Produced by TAJ Books International LLP

27, Ferndown Gardens,
Cobham,
Surrey,
UK,
KT11 2BH

www.tajbooks.com

Copyright ©2009 Taj Books International LLP

Copyright under International, Pan American, and Universal Copyright Conventions. All rights reserved. No part of this book may be reproduced or transmitted in any form or by any means, electronic or mechanical, including photocopying, recording, or by any information storage-and-retrieval system, without written permission from the copyright holder. Brief passages (not to exceed 1,000 words) may be quoted for reviews.

The Publishers wish to thank all of the manufacturers covered in this book for their cooperation in supplying photography. All images of Mirage 2000 and Rafale aircraft courtesy of Dassault Aviation.

All notations of errors or omissions (author inquiries, permissions) concerning the content of this book should be addressed to TAJ Books 27, Ferndown Gardens, Cobham, Surrey, UK, KT11 2BH, info@tajbooks.com.

ISBN-13: 978-1-906536-77-0

Printed in China.

FIGHTER AIRCRAFT

JAMES GIBB

Sandcastle Books

INTRODUCTION

Vickers F.B.5 Gunbus

The following is dedicated to the young men and women who flew these aircraft and in many cases gave their lives.

FIGHTER AIRCRAFT

A fighter aircraft is a military aircraft designed primarily for air-to-air combat with other aircraft, as opposed to a bomber, which is designed primarily to attack ground targets by dropping bombs. Fighters are small, fast, and manoeuverable. Fighter aircraft are the primary means by which armed forces gain air superiority over their opponents in battle. Since at least World War II, achieving and maintaining air superiority has been a key component of victory in warfare, particularly conventional warfare between regular armies.

TERMINOLOGY

The word "fighter" did not become the official English term for such aircraft until after World War I. In Great Britain's Royal Flying Corps – later the Royal Air Force – these aircraft continued to be called "scouts" into the early 1920s. The U.S. Army called their fighters "pursuit" aircraft from 1916 until the late 1940s. In the French and German languages the term used (and still in use) literally means "hunter". This has been followed in most other languages, an exception being Russian, in which the fighter is called "exterminator".

Although the term "fighter" technically refers to aircraft designed to shoot down other aircraft, such designs are often also useful as multirole fighter-bombers and sometimes lighter, fighter-sized tactical ground-attack aircraft.Fighters were developed in response to the fledgling use of aircraft and dirigibles in World War I for reconnaissance and ground-attack roles. Early fighters were very small and lightly armed by later standards, and were mostly biplanes. As aerial warfare became increasingly important, so did control of the airspace. By World War II, fighters were predominantly all-metal monoplanes with wing-mounted batteries of cannons or machine guns. By the end of the war, turbojet engines were already beginning to replace piston engines as the means of propulsion, and increasingly sophisticated refinements to armament were already appearing.

Airco DH.2

PISTON ENGINE FIGHTERS

World War I

The word "fighter" was first used to describe a two-seater aircraft with sufficient lift to carry a machine gun and its operator as well as the pilot. The first such "fighters" belonged to the "gunbus" series of experimental gun carriers of the British Vickers company which culminated in the Vickers F.B.5 Gunbus of 1914. The main drawback of this type of aircraft was its lack of speed. It was quickly realized that an aircraft intended to destroy its kind in the air needed at least to be fast enough to catch its quarry.

Fortunately another type of military aircraft already existed, which was to form the basis for an effective "fighter" in the modern sense of the word. It was based on the small fast aircraft developed before the war for such air races as the Gordon Bennett Cup and Schneider Trophy.

British "scout" aircraft in this sense included the Sopwith Tabloid and Bristol Scout; French equivalents included the light, fast Morane-Saulnier N.

In practice, soon after the actual commencement of the war, the pilots of small scout aircraft began to arm themselves with pistols, carbines, grenades, and an assortment of improvised weapons (even shotguns) with which to attack enemy aircraft. It was inevitable that sooner or later means of effectively arming "scouts" would be devised. One method was to build a "pusher" scout such as the Airco DH.2, with the propeller mounted behind the pilot. The main drawback was that the high drag of a pusher type's tail structure meant that it was bound to be slower than an otherwise similar "tractor" aircraft. The other approach was to mount the machine gun armament on a tractor-type airplane in a manner that enabled the gun to fire outside the arc of the propeller

Nevertheless, a machine gun firing over the propeller arc did have some advantages, and was to remain in service from 1915 (Nieuport 11) until 1918 (Royal Aircraft Factory S.E.5). The need to arm a tractor scout with a forward-firing gun whose bullets passed through the propeller arc was evident even before the outbreak of war, and its approach motivated inventors in both France and Germany to devise a practical synchronization gear that could time the firing of the individual rounds to when the propeller was not in the way. However, the synchronization gear (called the Zentralsteuerung in German) devised by

INTRODUCTION

Morane-Saulnier Type L

the engineers of Anthony Fokker's firm was the first gear to attract official sponsorship, and this would make the pioneering Fokker Eindecker monoplane a feared name over the Western Front, despite its being an adaptation of an obsolete pre-war French Morane-Saulnier racing airplane, with a mediocre performance and poor flight characteristics. The first victory for the Eindecker came on 1 July 1915, when Lieutenant Kurt Wintgens, flying with the Fliegerabteilung 6 unit on the Western Front, forced down a Morane-Saulnier Type L two-seat "parasol" monoplane of Luneville. Wintgens' aircraft, one of the five Fokker M.5K/MG production prototype examples of the Eindecker, was armed with a synchronized, air-cooled aviation version of the Parabellum MG14 machine gun, which did not require armored propellers.

The success of the Eindecker kicked off a competitive cycle of improvement among the combatants, building ever more capable single-seat fighters. The Albatros D.I of late 1916, designed by Robert Thelen, set the classic pattern followed by almost all such aircraft for about twenty years. Like the D.I, they were biplanes (only very occasionally occasionally monoplanes or triplanes).

The use of metal in fighter aircraft was pioneered in World War I by Germany, as Anthony Fokker used chrome-molybdenum steel tubing (a close chemical cousin to stainless steel) for the fuselage structure of all his fighter designs, and the innovative German engineer Hugo Junkers developed two all-metal, single-seat fighter monoplane designs with cantilever wings: the strictly experimental Junkers J 2 private-venture aircraft, made with steel, and some forty examples of the Junkers D.I, made with corrugated duralumin, all based on his pioneering Junkers J 1 all-metal airframe technology demonstration aircraft of late 1915.

INTERWAR PERIOD (1919-1938)

Fighter development slowed between the wars, with the most significant change coming late in the period, when the classic WWI type machines started to give way to metal monocoque or semi-monocoque monoplanes, with cantilever wing structures. Given limited defense budgets, air forces tended to be conservative in their aircraft purchases, and biplanes remained popular with pilots because of their agility. Designs such as the Gloster Gladiator, Fiat CR.42, and Polikarpov I-15 were common even in the late 1930s, and many were still in service as late as 1942. Up until the mid-1930s, the vast majority of fighter aircraft remained fabric-covered biplanes.

Fighter armament eventually began to be mounted inside the wings, outside the arc of the propeller, though most designs retained two synchronized machine-guns above the engine (which were considered more accurate).

The rotary engine, popular during WWI, quickly disappeared, replaced chiefly by the stationary radial engine. Aircraft engines increased in power several-fold over the period, going from a typical 180 hp (130 kW) in the 1918 Fokker D.VII to 900 hp (670 kW) in the 1938 Curtiss P-36.

The primary driver of fighter innovation, right up to the period of rapid rearmament in the late thirties, were not military budgets, but civilian aircraft races. Aircraft designed for these races pioneered innovations like streamlining and more powerful engines that would find their way into the fighters of World War II.

At the very end of the inter-war period came the Spanish Civil War. This was just the opportunity the German Luftwaffe, Italian Regia Aeronautica, and the Soviet Union's Red Air Force needed to test their latest aircraft designs. Each party sent several aircraft to back their side in the conflict. In the dogfights over Spain, the latest Messerschmitt fighters (Bf 109) did well, as did the Soviet Polikarpov I-16.

The Spanish Civil War also provided an opportunity for updating fighter tactics. One of the innovations to result from the aerial warfare experience this conflict provided was the development of the "finger-four" formation by the German pilot Werner Mölders.

Mitsubishi A6M Zero

WORLD WAR II

During the 1930s, two different streams of thought about air-to-air combat began to emerge, resulting in two different approaches to monoplane fighter development. In Japan and Italy especially, there continued to be a strong belief that lightly armed, highly maneuverable single-seat fighters would still play a primary role in air-to-air combat. Aircraft such as the Nakajima Ki-27, Nakajima Ki-43 and the Mitsubishi A6M Zero in Japan, and the Fiat G.50 and Macchi C.200 in Italy.

This Supermarine Spitfire XVI was typical of World War II fighters optimized for high level speeds and good climb rates

The other stream of thought, which emerged primarily in Britain, Germany, the Soviet Union, and the United States was the belief that the high speeds of modern combat aircraft and the g-forces imposed by aerial combat meant that dogfighting in the classic WWI sense would be impossible. Fighters such as the Messerschmitt Bf 109, the Supermarine Spitfire, the Yakovlev Yak-1 and the Curtiss P-40 Warhawk were all designed for high level speeds and a good rate of climb. Good maneuverability was desirable, but it was not the primary objective.

EUROPEAN THEATRE (WESTERN FRONT)

The Battle of Britain was the first major military campaign to be fought entirely by air forces, and it offered further lessons for both sides. Foremost was the value of radar for detecting and tracking enemy aircraft formations, which allowed quick concentration of fighters to intercept them farther from their targets.

The Battle of Britain also revealed inadequacies of extant tactical fighters when used for long-range strategic attacks. The twin-engined heavy fighter concept was revealed as a failed concept as the Luftwaffe's heavily armed but poorly maneuverable Messerschmitt Bf 110s proved highly vulnerable to nimble Hurricanes and Spitfires; the Bf 110s were subsequently relegated to night fighter and fighter-bomber roles for which they proved better-suited. Furthermore, the Luftwaffe's Bf 109s, operating near the limits of their range, lacked endurance for prolonged dogfighting over Britain.

The Allies themselves, however, would not learn this latter lesson until they sustained heavy bomber losses of their own during daylight raids against Germany. Despite the early assertions of strategic bombing advocates that "the bomber will always get through", even heavily armed U.S. Army Air Force (USAAF) bombers like the Boeing B-17 Flying Fortress and Consolidated B-24 Liberator suffered such high losses to German fighters (such as the Focke-Wulf Fw 190 "bomber destroyer") and anti-aircraft artillery (AAA) that – following the second raid on Schweinfurt in August 1943 – the U.S. Eighth Air Force was forced to suspend unescorted bombing missions into Germany until longer-range fighters became available for escort. These would appear in the form of Lockheed P-38 Lightnings, Republic P-47 Thunderbolts and North American P-51 Mustangs. As the war progressed, the growing numbers of these advanced, long-range fighters flown by pilots

INTRODUCTION

Bell P-39 Airacobra in flight firing all weapons at night

with increasing experience eventually overwhelmed their German opposition, despite the Luftwaffe's introduction of technological innovations like jet- and rocket-powered interceptors

European Theatre (Eastern Front)

On the Eastern Front, the strategic surprise of Operation Barbarossa demonstrated that Soviet air defense preparations were woefully inadequate. However, by the winter of 1941–1942, the Red Air Force was able to put together a cohesive air defense of Moscow, successfully interdict attacks on Leningrad, and begin production of new aircraft types in the relocated semi-built factories in the Urals, Siberia, Central Asia and the Caucasus. These facilities produced more advanced monoplane fighters, such as the Yak-1, Yak-3, LaGG-3, and MiG-3, to wrest air superiority from the Luftwaffe. Beginning in 1942, significant numbers of British, and later U.S., fighter aircraft were also supplied to aid the Soviet war effort, with the Bell P-39 Airacobra proving particularly effective in the lower-altitude combat typical of the Eastern Front.

Pacific Theatre

In the Pacific theatre, the experienced Japanese used their latest Mitsubishi A6M "Zero" to clear the skies of all opposition. Allied air forces – often flying obsolete aircraft, as the Japanese were not deemed as dangerous as the Germans – were caught off-guard and driven back until the Japanese became overextended.

Japanese fighter planes were also optimized for agility and range, and in time Allied airmen developed tactics that made better use of the superior armament and protection in their Grumman F4F Wildcats and Curtiss P-40s. From mid-1942, newer Allied fighter models were faster and better-armed than the Japanese fighters.

Technological innovations

Piston-engine power increased considerably during the war. The Curtiss P-36 Hawk had a 900 hp (670 kW) radial engine but was soon redesigned as the P-40 Warhawk with a 1100 hp (820 kW) in-line engine. By 1943, the latest P-40N had a 1300 hp (970 kW) Allison engine. At war's end, the German Focke-Wulf Ta 152 interceptor could achieve 2050 hp (1530 kW) with an MW-50 (methanol-

Curtiss P-40 "Warhawk"

water injection) supercharger and the American P-51H Mustang fitted with the Packard - V-1650-9 could achieve 2218 hp (1650 kW) under war emergency power. The Spitfire Mk I of 1939 was powered by a 1030 hp (770 kW) Merlin II; its 1945 successor, the Spitfire F.Mk 21, was equipped with the 2035 hp (1520 kW) Griffon 61. Likewise, the radial engines favoured for many fighters also grew from 1,100 hp (820 kW) to as much as 2090 hp (770 kW) during the same timeframe.

The first turbojet-powered fighter designs became operational in 1944, and clearly outperformed their piston-engined counterparts. New designs such as the Messerschmitt Me 262 and Gloster Meteor demonstrated the effectiveness of the new propulsion system. (Rocket-powered interceptors – most notable the Messerschmitt Me 163 – appeared at the same time, but proved less effective

More powerful armament became a priority early in the war, once it became apparent that newer stressed-skin monoplane fighters could not be easily shot down with rifle-caliber machine guns. Rapid technology advances in radar, which had been invented shortly prior to World War II, would permit their being fitted to some fighters, such as the Messerschmitt Bf 110, Bristol Beaufighter, de Havilland Mosquito, Grumman F6F Hellcat and Northrop P-61 Black Widow, to enable them to locate targets at night. The Germans developed several night-fighter types as they were under constant night bombardment by RAF Bomber Command. The British, who developed the first radar-equipped night fighters in 1940–1941, lost their technical lead to the Luftwaffe.

Post-World War II period

Several prototype fighter programs begun early in 1945 continued on after the war and led to advanced piston-engine fighters that entered production and operational service in 1946. A typical example is the Lavochkin La-9 'Fritz', which was an evolution of the successful wartime Lavochkin La-7 'Fin'. Working through a series of prototypes, the La-120, La-126 and La-130, the Lavochkin design bureau sought to replace the La-7's wooden airframe with a metal one, as well as fit a laminar-flow wing to improve maneuver performance, and increased armament. The La-9 entered service in August 1946 and was produced

INTRODUCTION

Messerschmitt Me 163B

until 1948; it also served as the basis for the development of a long-range escort fighter, the La-11 'Fang', of which nearly 1200 were produced 1947–1951. Over the course of the Korean War, however, it became obvious that the day of the piston-engined fighter was coming to a close and that the future would lie with the jet fighter.

This period also witnessed experimentation with jet-assisted piston engine aircraft. La-9 derivatives included examples fitted with two underwing auxiliary pulsejet engines (the La-9RD) and a similarly mounted pair of auxiliary ramjet engines (the La-138); however, neither of these entered service. One which did enter service – with the U.S. Navy in March 1945 – was the Ryan FR-1 Fireball; production was halted with the war's end on VJ-Day, with only 66 having been delivered, and the type was withdrawn from service in 1947. The USAAF had ordered its first 13 mixed turboprop-turbojet-powered pre-production prototypes of the Consolidated Vultee XP-81 Silver Bullet fighter, but this program was also canceled by VJ Day, with 80% of the engineering work completed.

ROCKET-POWERED FIGHTERS

The Messerschmitt Me 163 was the fastest aircraft of WWII and the only mass-produced rocket-powered fighter

The Saunders-Roe SR.53 was a successful design and was planned to be developed into production when economics forced curtailment of most British aircraft programs in the late 1950s. Furthermore, rapid advancements in jet engine technology had rendered mixed-power aircraft designs like Saunders-Roe's SR.53 (and its SR.177 maritime variant) obsolete. The American XF-91 Thunderceptor (which was the first U.S. fighter to exceed Mach 1 in level flight) met a similar fate for the same reason, and no hybrid rocket-and-jet-engine fighter design has ever been placed into service.

JET-POWERED FIGHTERS

It has become common in the aviation community to classify jet fighters by "generations" for historical purposes. There are no official definitions of these generations; rather, they represent the notion that there are stages in the development of fighter design approaches, performance capabilities, and technological evolution.

Lockheed P-80

First generation subsonic jet fighters (mid-1940s to mid-1950s)

The first generation of jet fighters comprises the initial, subsonic jet fighter designs introduced late in World War II and in the early post-war period. They differed little from their piston-engined counterparts in appearance, and many employed unswept wings. Guns remained the principal armament.

The first jets were developed during World War II and saw combat in its final year. Messerschmitt developed the first operational jet fighter, the Me 262. It was considerably faster than contemporary piston-driven aircraft, and in the hands of a competent pilot, was quite difficult for Allied pilots to defeat. The design was never deployed in numbers sufficient to stop the Allied air campaign, and a combination of fuel shortages, pilot losses, and technical difficulties with the engines kept the number of sorties low. Nevertheless, the Me 262 indicated the obsolescence of piston-driven aircraft. Spurred by reports of the German jets, Britain's Gloster Meteor entered production soon after and the two entered service around the same time in 1944. Despite their advantages, the early jet fighters were far from perfect, particularly in the opening years of the generation. Their operational lifespans could be measured primarily in hours; the engines themselves were fragile and bulky, and power could be adjusted only slowly. Many squadrons of piston-engined fighters were retained until the early-to-mid 1950s

The Americans were one of the first to begin using jet fighters post-war. The Lockheed P-80 Shooting Star (soon re-designated F-80) was less elegant than the swept-wing Me 262, but had a cruise speed (660 km/h [410 mph]) as high as the combat maximum of many piston-engined fighters. The British designed several new jets, including the iconic de Havilland Vampire which was sold to the air forces of many nations.

Ironically, the British transferred the technology of the Rolls-Royce Nene jet engine technology to the Soviets, who soon put it to use in their advanced Mikoyan-Gurevich MiG-15 fighters which were the first to introduce swept wings in combat, an innovation first proposed by German research which allowed flying much closer to the speed of sound than straight-winged designs such as the F-80. Their top speed of 1,075 km/h (668 mph) proved quite a shock to the American F-80 pilots who encountered them over

INTRODUCTION

Two US Navy Grumman F9F Panthers

Korea, along with their armament of two 23 mm cannons and a single 37 mm cannon compared to machine guns. The Americans responded by rushing their own swept-wing F-86 squadrons to battle against the MiGs which had similar trans-sonic performance. The two aircraft had different strengths, but were similar enough that the superior technology such as a radar ranging gunsight and skills and of the veteran United States Air Force pilots allowed them to prevail.

The world's navies also transitioned to jets during this period, despite the need for catapult-launching of the new aircraft. Grumman's F9F Panther was adopted by the U.S. Navy as their primary jet fighter in the Korean War period, and it was one of the first jet fighters to employ an afterburner. The de Havilland Vampire was the Royal Navy's first jet fighter. Radar was used on specialized night fighters such as the F3D Skyknight which also downed MiGs over Korea, and later fitted to the F2H Banshee and swept wing F7U Cutlass and F3H Demon as all-weather / night fighers

Second generation jet fighters (mid-1950s to early 1960s)

The development of second-generation fighters was shaped by technological breakthroughs, lessons learned from the aerial battles of the Korean War, and a focus on conducting operations in a nuclear warfare environment. Technological advances in aerodynamics, propulsion and aerospace building materials (primarily aluminium alloys) permitted designers to experiment with aeronautical innovations, such as swept wings, delta wings, and area-ruled fuselages. Widespread use of afterburning turbojet engines made these the first production aircraft to break the sound barrier, and the ability to sustain supersonic speeds in level flight became a common capability amongst fighters of this generation.

The prospect of a potential third world war featuring large mechanized armies and nuclear weapon strikes led to a degree of specialization along two design approaches: interceptors (like the English Electric Lightning and Mikoyan-Gurevich MiG-21F) and fighter-bombers (such as the Republic F-105 Thunderchief and the Sukhoi Su-7). Dogfighting, per se, was de-emphasized in both cases

F-15 Eagle

Third generation jet fighters (early 1960s to circa 1970)

The third generation witnessed continued maturation of second-generation innovations, but it is most marked by renewed emphases on maneuverability and traditional ground-attack capabilities Enhancements to improve the aerodynamic performance of third-generation fighters included flight control surfaces such as canards, powered slats, and blown flaps. A number of technologies would be tried for Vertical/Short Takeoff and Landing, but thrust vectoring would be successful on the Harrier jump jet.

Fourth generation jet fighters (circa 1970 to mid-1990s)

Fourth-generation fighters continued the trend towards multirole configurations, and were equipped with increasingly sophisticated avionics and weapon systems. Fighter designs were significantly influenced by the Energy-Maneuverability (E-M) theory developed by Colonel John Boyd and mathematician Thomas Christie. E-M characteristics were first applied to the F-15 Eagle, but Boyd and his supporters believed these performance parameters called for a small, lightweight aircraft with a larger, higher-lift wing.

The efforts of Boyd's "Fighter Mafia" would result in General Dynamics' (now Lockheed Martin's) F-16 Fighting Falcon.

The F-16's maneuverability was further enhanced by its being designed to be slightly aerodynamically unstable. This technique, called "relaxed static stability" (RSS), was made possible by introduction of the "fly-by-wire" (FBW) flight control system (FLCS), which in turn was enabled by advances in computers and system integration techniques. The F-16's sole reliance on electronics and wires to relay flight commands, instead of the usual cables and mechanical linkage controls, earned it the sobriquet of "the electric jet"

4.5th generation jet fighters (1990s to the present)

The end of the Cold War in 1989 led many governments to significantly decrease military spending as a "peace dividend". Air force inventories were cut, and research and

INTRODUCTION

development programs intended to produce what was then anticipated to be "fifth-generation" fighters took serious hits This opportunity enabled designers to develop fourth-generation designs – or redesigns – with significantly enhanced capabilities. These improved designs have become known as "Generation 4.5" fighters, recognizing their intermediate nature between the 4th and 5th generations, and their contribution in furthering development of individual fifth-generation technologies.

Prime examples of such aircraft, which are based on new airframe designs making extensive use of carbon-fibre composites, include the Eurofighter Typhoon, Dassault Rafale, Saab JAS 39 Gripen NG and the HAL Tejas.

Apart from these fighter jets, most of the 4.5 generation aircraft are actually modified variants of existing airframes from the earlier fourth generation fighter jets. Such fighter jets are generally heavier and examples include the Boeing F/A-18E/F Super Hornet which is an evolution of the 1970s F/A-18 Hornet design, the F-15E Strike Eagle which is a ground-attack variant of the Cold War-era F-15 Eagle, the Sukhoi Su-30MKI which is a further development of the Su-30 fighter and the Mikoyan MiG-29M/35, an upgraded version of the 1980s MiG-29. The Su-30MKI and MiG-35 use two- and three-dimensional thrust vectoring engines respectively so as to enhance maneuvering

FIFTH GENERATION JET FIGHTERS (2005 TO THE PRESENT)

The fifth generation was ushered in by the Lockheed Martin/Boeing F-22 Raptor in late 2005. Currently the cutting edge of fighter design, fifth-generation fighters are characterized by being designed from the start to operate in a network-centric combat environment, and to feature extremely low, all-aspect, multi-spectral signatures employing advanced materials and shaping techniques

Maneuver performance remains important and is enhanced by thrust-vectoring, which also helps reduce takeoff and landing distances. Supercruise may or may not be featured; it permits flight at supersonic speeds without the use of the afterburner – a device that significantly increases IR signature when used in full military power.

The expense of developing such sophisticated aircraft is as high as their capabilities. The U.S. Air Force had originally planned to acquire 650 F-22s, but it now appears that only about 200 will be built. As a result, its unit flyaway cost (FAC) is reported to be around $140 million.

To spread the development costs – and production base – more broadly, the Joint Strike Fighter (JSF) program enrolls eight other countries as cost- and risk-sharing partners. Altogether, the nine partner nations anticipate procuring over 3000 Lockheed Martin F-35 Lightning II fighters at an anticipated average FAC of $80-85 million. The F-35, however, is designed to be a family of three aircraft, a conventional take-off and landing (CTOL) fighter, a short take-off and vertical landing (STOVL) fighter, and a carrier-capable fighter, each of which has a different unit price. Other countries have initiated fifth-generation fighter development projects, with Russia's Sukhoi PAK-FA anticipated to enter service circa 2012–2015. In October 2007, Russia and India signed an agreement for joint participation in a Fifth-Generation Fighter Aircraft Program (FGFA), which will give India responsibility for development of a two-seat model of the PAK-FA. India is also developing its own indigenous fifth genration aircraft named Medium Combat Aircraft. China is reported to be pursuing multiple fifth-generation projects under the western code name; J-XX, and both Japan and South Korea have proposed indigenous programs.

FINALLY

In conclusion the design of fighter aircraft has always been at the cutting edge of several scientific disciplines. Aerodynamics, Structures, Materials and latterly Avionics. The first stainless steels were compounded for engine exhaust manifolds. The development of aluminium alloys for fuselage and wings. The invention and development of carbonfibre in its early years was totally concerned with aircraft engine components. The technology of extrusion for precision sections. The mathematical solutions to involved structural and aerodynamical problems; and the total involvement of computers both in design and the operation of aircraft.

It has been a long road from machines constructed of bamboo, birch, linen and piano wire to the modern aircraft made of materials that the early pioneers could only have dreamt about.

Right: The future of modern fighter aircraft. The X47-B Northrop Grumman unmanned fighter/bomber

A-10 Thunderbolt

The A-10 was developed in response to the increasing vulnerability of ground attack-planes as evidenced by the large number that were shot down to small arms fire, surface-to-air missiles, and low level anti-aircraft gunfire during the Vietnam War. This led to a need for a specialized, heavily armed, heavily armored aircraft. Previous aircraft used in the CAS mission had been bombers or fighters pressed into the job.

On 6 March 1967 the US Air Force released a request for information to 21 companies. Their objective was to create a design study for a low cost attack aircraft designated A-X, or "Attack Experimental". In May 1970, the USAF issued a modified, yet much more detailed request for proposals (RFP). Six companies submitted contestants to the USAF, with Northrop and Fairchild Republic selected to build prototypes: the YA-9A and YA-10A, respectively.

First flight of the A-10 was in May 1972. After trials and a flyoff against the A-9, the Air Force selected Fairchild-Republic's A-10 as the winner on 10 January 1973. The first production A-10 flew in October 1975, and deliveries to the Air Force commenced in March 1976. The first squadron to use the A-10 went operational in October 1977. 715 aircraft were produced, ending in 1984.

The A-10/OA-10 has excellent maneuverability at low speeds and altitude, thanks to wide, straight wings. These also allow short takeoffs and landings, permitting operations from airfields near front lines. The plane can loiter for extended periods of time and operate under 1,000 foot (300 m) ceilings with 1.5-mile (2.4 km) visibility. It can fly at a relatively slow speed of 200 mph (320 km/h), which makes it better at ground-attack than fast fighter-bombers, which often have difficulty targeting small and slow-moving targets.

The 'Warthog' is exceptionally hardy, with a strong airframe that can survive direct hits from armor-piercing and high-explosive projectiles up to 23 mm. The aircraft has triple redundancy in its flight systems, with mechanical systems to back up double-redundant hydraulic systems. This permits pilots to fly and land when hydraulic power or part of a wing is lost. The aircraft is designed to fly with one engine and a wing torn off. Self-sealing fuel tanks are protected by fire-retardant foam. Additionally, the main landing gear is designed so that the wheels semi-protrude from their nacelles when the gear is retracted so as to make gear-up landings (belly landing) easier to control and less damaging to the aircraft's underside.

AV8B *Harrier*

The AV-8B had its direct origins in a Joint U.S.-British project (Hawker-Siddeley and McDonnell Douglas Aircraft) for a much-improved Harrier aircraft, to be the AV-16A Advanced Harrier program. However cost over-runs in engine development on the part of Rolls Royce and in the aircraft development caused the British to pull out of the program. Interest remained in the U.S. so a less ambitious, though still expensive project was undertaken by McDonnell on their own catered to U.S. needs. Using things learned from AV-16A development, though dropping some things such as further Pegasus development, the development work continued leading the AV-8B for the U.S. Marine Corps. The aircraft was centered on the Marine's needs, light ground attack and was focused on payload and range as opposed to speed. In the late 1970 the British re-entered development of their own second generation Harrier based on the U.S. design leading eventually to the GR.5, which had somewhat different performance goals.

Aircraft were built by McDonnell Douglas and BAE Systems the latter at their Kingston & Dunsfold facilities in Surrey, in the UK. The factorys were also home to the Hawker Hunter, & BAe Hawk T1.

The aircraft is known mainly as the AV-8B in USMC service and the GR7/GR9 in RAF service. The AV-8A (and also TAV-8A versions) , which was the previous generation of Harrier and should not be confused with the next generation, was a Hawker-Siddeley Harrier GR.3 procured for the US Marine Corps.

While the Harrier is one of the most flexible aircraft ever made, the necessary understanding and skill to pilot it are considerable. In addition to being able to fly the Harrier in forward flight (above stall speed when it behaves in the manner of a typical fixed-wing aircraft), it is necessary to maintain control during VTOL and STOL manouvres when the lift and control surfaces don't work. This requires skills and understanding more associated with helicopters. Most services demand great aptitude and extensive training, with experience of piloting both types of aircraft. Many recruit trainee pilots from the most experienced and skilled helicopter pilots in their organisations.

DASSAULT Mirage 2000

The Mirage 2000 is a French-built multi-role fighter manufactured by Dassault Aviation. The true origin of the Mirage 2000 is the less-known Mirage 4000, a twin engine delta air interceptor that was a private venture from Dassault, and was very capable. The Royal Saudi Air Force was very interested, but eventually it dropped from the project in favor of the American F-15. As a result of this lost sale, Dassault built a scaled down, less expensive, but still very capable version of the 4000: the Mirage 2000. Its first role is to be an interceptor, yet it retains a ground-attack capability. Using only the basic concept of the delta interceptor previously seen on the classic Mirage III, Dassault built a totally new design. Using fly-by-wire controls and relaxed stability, Dassault was capable of bringing the classic delta to a new level, with loads up to 12g's (for short periods of time, the default is 9g's), a more powerful engine (but not so powerful as the latest American engines, an old problem the French aircraft industries were still not able to overcome). Development began on the aircraft in the 1970s and the first flight took place in 1978. By 1983 it began seeing service in the French Air Force. The Mirage 2000 has many variants. The first operational Mirage 2000 was the 2000C, using first the stopgap RDM radar, and later the definitive RDI digital radar. The evolution of the 2000 came with the Mirage 2000-5, with much improved RDY radar, glass cockpit, MICA fire-and-forget BVR missiles and numerous other improvements. The Mirage 2000 has a maximum speed of Mach 2.2. More than 500 have been produced.

The Mirage 2000 serves the air forces of Egypt, France, Greece, India, Peru, Qatar, Republic of China (Taiwan), United Arab Emirates and is currently the front-line fighter for the French Air Force (Armée de l'Air). After the French Air Force, the Indian Air Force (IAF) fields the greatest number of Mirage 2000 aircraft. In 2005, the IAF expressed its desire to purchase about 200 Mirage 2000-5 aircraft. However, Dassault backed out Mirage from the race and instead offered the sale of Dassault Rafale claiming the latter to be much more suited for Indian needs.

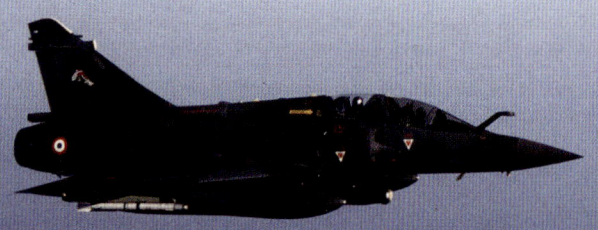

DASSAULT *Rafale*

The Rafale is a French twin-engined delta-wing highly agile multi-role fighter aircraft designed and built by Dassault Aviation. Introduced in 2000, the Rafale is produced both for land-based use with the French Air Force and for carrier-based naval operations with the French Navy.

In the mid-1970s, both the French Air Force and Navy had a requirement to find a new generation of fighter, and their requirements were similar enough to be merged into one project. Dassault considered cooperating in the development of the aircraft that was eventually called the Eurofighter Typhoon but the French government cited the need to field an aircraft sooner than Eurofighter.

The Rafale features a delta wing combined with active integrated (Close-coupled) canard to maximize maneuverability (withstanding +9g or -3g) while maintaining stability in flight, a maximum of 11g can be reached in case of emergency. The canard also reduces landing speed to 115 knots. According to internal sources, the low speed limit is 100kt but 80kt is sometimes demonstrated during airshows by pilots willing to underline low speed qualities of the aircraft. A minimum of 15 kt have been reached during simulated combat vs a Mirage 2000 by an aggressive pilot. The aircraft can operate from 400 meter runways.

Initial deliveries of the Rafale M were to the F1 ("France 1") standard. This meant that the aircraft was suitable for air-to-air combat, replacing the obsolescent F-8 Crusader as the Aviation Navale's carrier-based fighter, but not equipped or armed for air-to-ground operations. Actual deliveries (to Flotille 11 some time after 2007) are to the "F2" standard, giving air-to-ground capability, and replacing the Dassault-Breguet Super Étendard in the ground attack role and the Dassault Étendard IVP in the reconnaissance role. This will leave the Rafale M as the only fixed-wing combat aircraft flown by the Aviation Navale, and plans are to upgrade all airframes to the "F3" standard, with terrain-following 3D radar and nuclear capability, from early in the decade following 2010.

38

EUROFIGHTER *Typhoon*

The Eurofighter Typhoon is a twin-engine multi-role canard-delta strike fighter aircraft, designed and built by a consortium of European aerospace manufacturers, Eurofighter GmbH, formed in 1986.

The series production of the Eurofighter Typhoon is underway, and the aircraft is being procured under three separate contracts (referred to as "tranches"), each for aircraft with generally improved capabilities. The aircraft has entered service with the British Royal Air Force, the German Luftwaffe, the Italian Air Force, the Spanish Air Force and the Austrian Air Force. Saudi Arabia has signed a £4.43 billion contract for 72 aircraft.

The Typhoon features foreplanes, and lightweight construction. The fighter achieves high agility at both supersonic and low speeds by having a relaxed stability design. It has a quadruplex digital fly-by-wire control system providing artificial stability, as manual operation alone could not compensate for the inherent instability. The fly-by-wire system is described as "carefree" by preventing the pilot from exceeding the permitted manoeuvre envelope.

Although not designated a stealth fighter, measures were taken to reduce the Typhoon's radar cross section (RCS), especially from the frontal aspect. An example of these measures is that the Typhoon has jet inlets that conceal the front of the jet engine (a strong radar target) from radar. Many important potential radar targets, such as the wing, canard and fin leading edges, are highly swept, so will reflect radar energy well away from the front sector. Some external weapons are mounted semi-recessed into the aircraft, partially shielding these missiles from incoming radar waves. In addition radar absorbent materials (RAM) developed primarily by EADS/DASA coat many of the most significant reflectors. The Typhoon's current Euroradar CAPTOR radar is relatively easy to detect when operating, unlike a few more advanced radars. For that reason the Eurofighter operates automatic Emission Controls (EMCON) to reduce the Electro-Magnetic emissions of the Radar.

F-2 *Defense Fighter*

The Mitsubishi F-2 is a Japanese fighter aircraft manufactured by Mitsubishi. It is based on the Lockheed Martin F-16 and that company is a major subcontractor to Mitsubishi.

In October 1987, Japan selected the F-16 as the basis of its new fighter, to replace the Mitsubishi F-1. The F-2 programme has been controversial, because the unit cost is roughly 4 times that of a Block 50/52 F-16. It has been argued that this demonstrates Japan's commitment to its aerospace industry.

Some differences in the F-2 from the F-16 include, a 25% larger wing area radar absorbent materials on the leading edges, a longer nose to accommodate a phased-array radar and a larger tailplane.

The F-2's maiden flight was on October 7, 1995. Later that year, the Japanese government approved an order for 130, to enter service by 1999; structural problems resulted in service entry being delayed until 2001.

Because of issues with cost-efficiency, orders for the aircraft were severely curtailed in 2004.

Earlier version of F-16 is USD 25 m, an F-2 is probably about USD 100 m (However the UAE paid 8 billion US-Dollar for 80 F-16 Block 60, so if all cost are combined the F-2 and the latest version of the F-16 are not that far away.)

The F-2 Defense Fighter has a 20 mm JM61A1 cannon, plus a maximum weapon load of 8,085 kg. This can include various load-outs, including the air-to-air missiles, AIM-9 Sidewinder, AIM-7 Sparrow, Mitsubishi AAM-3, Mitsubishi AAM-4. Air-to-ground weapons including, the ASM-1 and ASM-2 anti-ship missiles, and various free-fall bombs with GCS-1 IIR seeker heads, and JDAM.

F-15 *Eagle*

The Boeing (formerly McDonnell Douglas) F-15 Eagle is an American-built all-weather tactical fighter designed to gain and maintain air superiority in aerial combat. It first flew in July of 1972. A derivative of the aircraft is the F-15E Strike Eagle, a highly successful all-weather strike fighter which entered service in 1988.

The F-15's maneuverability is derived from low wing loading (weight to wing area ratio) with a high thrust-to-weight ratio enabling the aircraft to turn tightly without losing airspeed. The F-15 can climb to 30,000 ft. in around 60 seconds. The weapons and flight control systems are designed so one person can safely and effectively perform air-to-air combat.

The F-15's versatile APG-63/70 Pulse-doppler radar system can look up at high-flying targets and down at low-flying targets without being confused by ground clutter. It can detect and track aircraft and small high-speed targets at distances beyond visual range down to close range, and at altitudes down to treetop level. The radar feeds target information into the central computer for effective weapons delivery. For close-in dogfights, the radar automatically acquires enemy aircraft, and this information is projected on the head-up display. The F-15's electronic warfare system provides both threat warning and automatic countermeasures against selected threats. Because of the advanced electronics deployed on the F-15, the aircraft was given the nickname "Starship" by users. When the pilot changes from one weapon system to another, visual guidance for the required weapon automatically appears on the head-up display.

The F-15E Strike Eagle is a two-seat, dual-role, totally integrated fighter for all-weather, air-to-air and deep interdiction missions. The rear cockpit is upgraded to include four multi-purpose CRT displays for aircraft systems and weapons management. The digital, triple-redundant Lear Siegler flight control system permits coupled automatic terrain following, enhanced by a ring-laser gyro inertial navigation system.

For low-altitude, high-speed penetration and precision attack on tactical targets at night or in adverse weather, the F-15E carries a high-resolution APG-70 radar and low-altitude navigation and targeting infrared for night pods.

F-16 *Fighting Falcon*

The F-16 Fighting Falcon is a modern multi-role jet fighter, developed by General Dynamics in the United States. Initially designed as a lightweight fighter, the plane has evolved into a successful multi-role aircraft. The Falcon's versatility is the primary reason that it is success on the export market, currently serving 24 countries. It is the largest and probably most significant Western fighter program, with over 4000 aircraft built. Though no longer produced for the United States Air Force, it is still produced for export.

The F-16 originated in a set of specifications by the United States Department of Defense. The deficiencies of the F-4 Phantom II in aerial combat in the Vietnam War, particularly at close ranges, shaped the specifications for the F-15 Eagle. An informal and influential group nicknamed the "Fighter Mafia", among them systems analyst Pierre Sprey, test pilot Charles E. Meyers, test pilot Everest Riccioni, and former instructor pilot John Boyd, believed the F-15 was a move in the wrong direction. They argued that the F-15 was too large and expensive. Designed as a fast interceptor, it had a wide turn radius and was not well suited to close range dogfighting. The Fighter Mafia argued for a lighter fighter with superb maneuverability, that was cheap enough to deploy in numbers. These specifications became the Lightweight Fighter (LWF) program, begun in 1971.

The Fighting Falcon is regarded as a superb dogfighter, with innovations such as the bubble canopy, side-mounted control stick, and reclined seat. It was also the first US fighter aircraft to match the English Electric Lightning's ability to execute 9 g turns. Although the F-16's official popular name is "Fighting Falcon", it is known to its pilots as the "Viper", the General Dynamics codename for the project during its early development.

The F-16 is a single engine, multi-mission tactical aircraft. It is equipped with an M61 Vulcan cannon in the left wing root, and can be equipped with air-to-air missiles and a large variety of missiles or bombs.

From the very beginning, the F-16 was intended to be a cost-effective "workhorse," that could perform various kinds of missions and maintain around-the-clock readiness. It is much simpler and lighter than its predecessors, but uses advanced aerodynamics and avionics (including the first use of fly-by-wire, earning it the nickname of "the electric jet") to maintain good performance.

58

59

F-22 Raptor

The F-22 Raptor is a stealth fighter aircraft built by Lockheed Martin Aeronautics and Boeing Integrated Defense Systems. It was originally envisioned as an air superiority fighter, but is equipped for ground attack, electronic attack, and signals intelligence roles as well.

The Raptor's combat computer systems and power are unmatched by any other fighter planned to be developed by 2020. The AN/APG-77 AESA radar, designed for air-superiority and strike operations, features a low-observable, active-aperture, electronically-scanned array that can track multiple targets in all kinds of weather. The AN/APG-77 changes frequencies more than 1,000 times per second to reduce the chance of being intercepted. The radar can also focus its emissions to overload enemy sensors, giving the plane an electronic-attack capability.

The radar's information is processed by the two Raytheon-built Common Integrated Processor (CIP)s. Each CIP operates at 10.5 billion instructions per second and has 300 megabytes of memory. Unprecedented amounts of information can be gathered from the radar and other onboard and offboard systems, filtered by the CIP, and offered in easy-to-digest ways on several cockpit displays, enabling the pilot to remain on top of complicated situations. The Raptor's software is composed of over 1.7 million lines of code, most of which concerns processing data from the radar.

Although several recent Western fighters have had measures introduced to make them less detectable on radar, such as radar absorbent material coated S shaped intake ducts that shield the compressor fan from reflecting radar waves, the F-22A design has placed a much higher degree of importance on making the plane hard to detect than has previously been seen in fighter designs.

The Raptor is designed to carry air-to-air missiles in internal bays to avoid disrupting its stealth capability. Missiles are launched by hydraulic arms that hurl them away from the jet so quickly that the weapons-bay doors pop open for less than one second. The plane can also carry bombs such as the large JDAM and the new Small-Diameter Bomb. It can carry non-stealthy weapons on four external hardpoints, but this vastly increases the plane's radar signature. The Raptor carries a General Electric M61A2 Vulcan 20 mm Gatling cannon, also with a trap door, in the right wing root.

F-35 *Joint Strike Fighter*

The JSF exists in three primary variants. The F-35A, F-35B, and F-35C. For the JSF Trials, only the F-35A and F-35B models were demonstrated. The F-35A is the smallest, lightest version, which uses conventional takeoff and landing. The F-35A variant is intended for use primarily by the U.S. Air Force. The F-35C is the largest F-35, with the largest wingspan and the heaviest, most reinforced fuselage. The F-35C is intended for use as a carrier based aircraft, the larger wing area allowing more control at low carrier landing velocities and high glide angles, and the reinforced fuselage required for the extremes of carrier arrested landings and catapult launches. The final F-35 variant is the F-35B VSTOL aircraft, often referred to as the F-35 Marine version. The F-35B is clearly intended to replace the U.S. Marine Corps' AV-8B Harrier strike jets, while retaining common parts with other F-35 aircraft. F-35B is capable of vertical take-off and landing.

The F-35 powerplant uses the highly complex Remote Shaft-Driven Lift Fan concept. Turbine power is diverted forward via a clutch-and-bevel gearbox, to a vertically mounted, contra-rotating lift fan located forward of the main engine in the center of the aircraft. Bypass air from the turbofan exhausts through a pair of roll post nozzles on either side of the fuselage, while both the lift fan and the LP turbine streams exhaust through thrust vectoring nozzles. In effect, the F-35 power plant acts as a flow multiplier and consequently has more than sufficient thrust for lift operations. This lift concept has the additional benefit of lowering environmental effects during (primarily) landing, where the thermal effects on, for example, a carrier deck are greatly reduced.

The rival Boeing X-32 adopted the Direct Lift System, where the engine exhaust gases were redirected to thrust vectoring nozzles to achieve lift during a STOVL landing. However, even though the fan was oversized and throttle-pushed, it was said to suffer insufficient thrust for lift. Because of the large required engine airflow, the X-32 had a large front air intake, compromising the aesthetics and the aircraft's aerodynamics. According to critics, Boeing designed an airplane "only its mother would love", in violation of the maxim "if it looks good, it flies good".

Arguably the most persuasive demonstration of the F-35's capability was the final qualifying flight of the JSF Trials, wherein the F-35B STOVL aircraft traveled in excess of Mach 1 for a duration, and then performed a vertical landing.

FA-18 *Hornet*

The F/A-18 Hornet is a modern all-weather carrier strike fighter. Designed in the 1970s, the plane is in service with the U.S. Navy and U.S. Marine Corps, as well as many other armed forces across the globe. It fills the roles of fighter escort, fleet air defense, suppression of enemy air defenses (SEAD), interdiction, close and deep air support, reconnaissance, and forward air control. Its versatility and reliability have proven it to be a valuable carrier asset. Its drawbacks include its relative lack of range and speed, and its inability to land on aircraft carriers with significant combat loads.

The F/A-18 is a twin engine, mid-wing, multi-mission tactical aircraft. It is superbly maneuverable, owing to its good thrust to weight ratio, digital fly-by-wire control system, and leading edge extensions (LEX). The LEX allow the Hornet to remain controllable at high angles of attack. This is because the LEX produce powerful vortices over the wings, creating turbulent airflow and thus delaying or eliminating the aerodynamic separation responsible for stall.

The Hornet was among the first aircraft to heavily utilize multi-function displays, which at the switch of a button allow the pilot to perform either fighter or attack roles or both. This "force multiplier" capability gives the operational commander more flexibility in employing tactical aircraft in a rapidly changing battle scenario. It was the first Navy aircraft to incorporate a digital multiplex avionics bus, enabling easy upgrades.

The Hornet is also notable for having been designed with maintenance in mind, and as a result has required far less downtime than its counterparts, the F-14 Tomcat and the A-6 Intruder. Its mean time between failure is three times greater than any other Navy strike aircraft, and requires half the maintenance time. For example, whereas replacing the engine on the A-4 Skyhawk required removing the aircraft's tail, the engine on the Hornet is attached at only three points and can be directly removed without excessive disassembly.

83

85

MIG 29

The MiG-29, like the larger Sukhoi Su-27 'Flanker', began development in 1969, when the Soviet Union learned of the U.S. Air Force 'FX' program, which would eventually produce the F-15 Eagle. Even before the aircraft was developed, Soviet leadership realized that the new American fighter would represent a serious technological advance over all existing Soviet fighters. The MiG-21 'Fishbed' had been agile by the standards of its day, but its size left it deficient in range, armament, and growth potential. The MiG-23 'Flogger', developed to match the F-4 Phantom II, was fast and had more space for fuel and equipment, but its maneuverability and dog fighting ability were deficient. The Soviets clearly needed a better-balanced fighter with both agility and sophisticated systems.

In response, the Soviet General Staff issued a requirement for a Perspektivnyi Frontovoi Istrebitel (PFI, roughly 'advanced tactical fighter'). It was extremely ambitious, calling for long range, good short-field performance (including the ability to use austere runways), excellent agility, Mach 2+ speed, and heavy armament. The aerodynamic design for the new aircraft was largely carried out by TsAGI, the Russian aerodynamics institute, in collaboration with Sukhoi.

In 1971 the Soviets determined that the PFI aircraft would be too expensive to procure in the quantities needed (directly paralleling the contemporary USAF experience that led to the Lightweight Fighter program and the F-16 Fighting Falcon and YF-17 Cobra), and divided it into TPFI (Tyazholyi Perspektivnyi Frontovoi Istrebitel, heavy advanced tactical fighter) and LPFI (Legkiy Perspektivnyi Frontovoi Istrebitel, lightweight advanced tactical fighter). The heavy fighter remained with Sukhoi (resulting in the Su-27 'Flanker'), while the lightweight fighter went to Mikoyan.

The resultant Product 9, designated MiG-29A, began detail design work in 1974. The first flight took place 6 October 1977. The preproduction aircraft was first spotted by United States reconnaissance satellites in November of that year; it was dubbed Ram-L because the U.S. knew only that it was being built at the Zhukovsky flight test centre near the town of Ramenskoye. Early western speculation suggested that the Ram-L would be very similar in appearance to the YF-17 Cobra and would be powered by afterburning Tumansky R-25 turbojets. The MiG-29 was first publicly seen in the West during a visit to Finland in July 1986.

MIG 31

Like its MiG-25 predecessor, the MiG-31 was surrounded by early speculation and misinformation concerning its design and capabilities. The West learned of the new interceptor from Lieutenant Viktor Belenko, a pilot who defected to Japan in 1976 with his MiG-25P. Belenko described an upcoming "Super Foxbat" with two seats and a capability to intercept cruise missiles. According to his testimony, the new interceptor was to have air intakes similar to the MiG-23 'Flogger', which the MiG-31 in reality does not have, at least not in production variants. While undergoing testing, a MiG-31 was spotted by a reconnaissance satellite at the Zhukovsky flight test center near the town of Ramenskoye. The images were interpreted as a fixed-wing interceptor version of a swing-wing fighter codenamed the "Ram-K". The latter was eventually revealed to be the Sukhoi Su-27 'Flanker', a wholly unrelated design.

Series production of the MiG-31 began in 1979, with operational models entering Soviet Anti-Air Defense (PVO) service in 1982. It was first photographed by a Norwegian pilot over the Barents Sea in 1985.

The MiG-31 was sought after for a variety of long-range missions. Following the collapse of the USSR, however, the budget for spares (MIG31 AOG desk was created to solve this problem) and maintenance collapsed, leaving many squadrons unable to maintain their complex aircraft. By 1996, only 20% of remaining aircraft were reportedly serviceable at any time; however, by early 2006, a stronger Russian economy permitted the return to service of around 75% of the Russian Air Force's (VVS') MiG-31s.

About 500 MiG-31s were produced, approximately 370 of which remain in Russian service, with another 30 or so in Kazakhstan. Some upgrade programs have found their way in the MiG-31 fleet, like the MiG-31BM multirole version with upgraded avionics, new multimode radar, hands-on-throttle-and-stick (HOTAS) controls, liquid-crystal (LCD) color multi-function displays (MFDs), ability to carry the AA-12 'Adder' missile and various Russian air-to-ground missiles (AGMs) such as the AS-17 'Krypton' anti-radiation missile (ARM), a new and more powerful computer, and digital datalinks. However, only very small number of Russian aircraft have been upgraded to the MiG-31BM standard, although others have been equipped with new computer and the ability to carry the R-77 long-range missile as well.

PANAVIA *Tornado*

The Panavia Tornado is a family of twin-engine combat aircraft, which was jointly developed by the United Kingdom, West Germany and Italy. There are three primary versions of the Tornado; the Tornado IDS (Interdictor/Strike) fighter-bomber, the suppression of enemy air defences Tornado ECR (Electronic Combat/ Reconnaissance) and the Tornado ADV (Air Defence Variant) interceptor. It is one of the world's most sophisticated and capable interdiction and attack aircraft, with a large payload, long range and high survivability.

Developed and built by Panavia, a tri-national consortium consisting of British Aerospace (previously British Aircraft Corporation), MBB of West Germany, and Alenia Aeronautica of Italy, the Tornado first flew on August 14, 1974, and saw action with the RAF, AMI (Italian Air Force) and Royal Saudi Air Force in the Gulf War.

The Tornado was designed as a low-level supersonic ground attack bomber, capable of taking off and landing in short distances. This requires good high-speed and low-speed flying characteristics. In general, an aircraft which is designed to fly at high speeds usually has poor low-speed characteristics. In order to achieve the desired high-speed performance, an aircraft has a highly swept or 'delta' wing platform. However, these wing designs are very inefficient at low speeds where unswept wing planforms are required. In order for an aircraft to be operated efficiently at both high and low speeds, variable wing sweep is a desirable feature; this was incorporated into the Tornado design.

When the wings are swept back, the Tornado IDS increases its high-speed low-level capability by reducing drag. When sweeping, the wings partially slide into the fuselage, reducing the exposed wing area. This gives the aircraft a low gust response in turbulent low-level winds. This not only makes flight much more comfortable for the aircrew but also makes the aircraft a more stable platform from which to aim and deliver unguided weapons at low level.

The aircraft was designed to be land-based and operate from large airfields that were considered to be vulnerable to aerial attack. Therefore, during the development of the aircraft, short field landing capability was considered essential in order to enable the aircraft to operate from short strips on potentially damaged runways and taxiways.

96

SAAB *Gripen*

The Saab JAS 39 Gripen (Translated in English as Griffin) is a fighter aircraft manufactured by the Swedish aerospace company Saab. Gripen International acts as a prime contracting organisation and is responsible for marketing, selling and supporting the Gripen fighter around the world.

The aircraft is in service with the Swedish Air Force, the Czech Air Force, the Hungarian Air Force and the South African Air Force, and has been ordered by the Royal Thai Air Force. A total of 236 Gripens have been ordered as of 2008.

One interesting feature is the Gripen's ability to take off and land on public roads, which was part of Sweden's war defence strategy. The aircraft is designed to be able to operate even if the air force does not have air superiority.

During the Cold War, the Swedish Armed Forces were preparing to defend against a possible invasion from the Soviet Union. Even though the defensive strategy in principle called for an absolute defence of Swedish territory, military planners calculated that Swedish defence forces could eventually be overrun. For that reason, Sweden had military stores dispersed all over the country, in order to maintain the capacity of inflicting damage on the enemy even if military installations were lost.

Accordingly, among the requirements from the Swedish Air Force was that the Gripen fighter should be able to land on public roads near military stores for quick maintenance, and take off again. As a result, the Gripen fighter can be refueled and re-armed in ten minutes by a five man mobile ground crew operating out of a truck, and then resume flying sorties.[24]

In the post-Cold War era, these dispersed operation capabilities have proved to be of great value for a different purpose. The Gripen fighter system is expeditionary in nature, and therefore well suited for peace-keeping missions worldwide, which has become the new main task of the Swedish Armed Forces.

The cockpit has three full colour head down displays and digital emergency instrument presentation unique to the aircraft. The cockpit layout provides a human-machine interface that eases pilot workload substantially and increases situational awareness, but still provides substantial future growth potential. The pilot flies the aircraft by means of a centre stick and left hand throttles.

SUKHOI *SU-27*

The Sukhoi Su-27 (NATO reporting name 'Flanker') is originally a Soviet fighter aircraft designed by the Sukhoi Design Bureau (SDB). It was intended as a direct competitor for the new generation of American fighters (which emerged as the F-14 Tomcat, F-15 Eagle, F-16 Fighting Falcon, and F/A-18 Hornet), with exceptional range, heavy armament, and very high agility. The Su-27 most often flies air superiority missions, but is able to perform almost all combat operations. Some believe the Su-27 to have been born from a competition between Sukhoi and Mikoyan-Gurevich, given the Su-27's and Mikoyan MiG-29's similar shape. This is not so. The Su-27 was designed as long-range air superiority fighter and interceptor, whereas the MiG-29 was designed to fill the role of short-range tactical support fighter.

The Su-33 Fleet Defense Interceptor was developed from the Su-27 design for use on aircraft carriers. Main differences include a tail hook and canards. Given the purpose of this interceptor, one would say that its closest counterpart is the American F-14 Tomcat, whereas the Mikoyan-Gurevich MiG-29K would be analogous to the F/A-18 Hornet.

The Su-30 is a two-seat, dual-role, fighter for all-weather, air-to-air and deep interdiction missions.

Further versions include the Su-34 strike variant and the Su-35 improved air defence fighter.

The Su-27's basic design is aerodynamically similar to the MiG-29, but it is substantially larger. It is a very large aircraft, and to mimimize its weight its structure has a high percentage of titanium (about 30%, more than any of its contemporaries). No composite materials were used. The swept wing blends into the fuselage at the leading edge extensions and is essentially a delta, although the tips are cropped for wingtip missile rails or ECM pods. The Su-27 is not a true delta, however, because it retains conventional tailplanes, with two vertical tailfins outboard of the engines, supplemented by two fold-down ventral fins for additional lateral stability.

The Su-27's Lyulka AL-31F turbofan engines are widely spaced, both for safety reasons and to ensure uninterrupted airflow through the intakes. The space between the engines also provides additional lift, reducing wing loading. Movable guide vanes in the intakes allow Mach 2+ speeds, and help to maintain engine airflow at high alpha. A mesh screen over each intake prevents debris from being drawn into the engines during take-off.

SUKHOI SU-35

The Sukhoi Su-35 is a 4.5 generation heavy class, long-range, multi-role, air superiority fighter and strike fighter. Due to the similar features and components it contains, the Sukhoi Su-35 is considered to be a close cousin of the Sukhoi Su-30MKI, a specialized version of the Su-30. It has been further developed into the Su-35BM. The Su-35 is in service in small numbers with the Russian Air Force with 12 in service as of 2008.

Sukhoi began modernizing the Su-35 in the mid-2000s to provide a 4.5 type generation fighter making use of current technologies. The modernised Su-35 will be interim design until the fifth generation PAK FA (T-50) enters service. The first modernised Su-35 was presented at the MAKS-2007 air show in August 2007.

The new Su-35 omits the canards and speedbrake flap from the original Su-35 design. It also has a reinforced airframe for longer service life which creates a reduced radar signature from the front. The modernised Su-35's new nose holds an improved passive electronically scanned array radar and the aircraft features many other upgrades to its avionics and electronic systems, including digital fly-by-wire and a rear-looking radar for firing Semi-Active Radar missiles. A two-dimensional asymmetric thrust vectoring system was tested on the Su-35 and seems to be the basis for the development of the Su-37. A new type of 2D thrust vectoring engine, the 117S, has been developed and replaces the current AL-31F or AL-35. The modernised Su-35's radar has an average power output of 5 kW and a peak output of 20 kW. When the H035 radar was tested on Su-30MK No. 503, the detection range was as far as 290 kilometers with 1 kW power output. The radar system can track up to 30 aerial targets and engage up to eight.

The plane reverts back to a canard-less configuration, contrary to the designs of Sukhoi's other recent machines-the Su-30MKI and the Su-37. The canards were needed to increase/maintain maneuverability of the planes despite the addition of more modern, significantly heavier (than Su-27) hardware in the nose area. The disadvantage of canards is that they significantly increase drag, thus decreasing efficiency, speed, range, and weapons-carrying capacity. The Su-35 uses composite materials and newer on board electronic packages to make the insides of the aircraft significantly lighter, especially in the nose area. This allowed the designers at Sukhoi to do away with the Canards and their disadvantages while still keeping up high operational system characteristics.

INDEX

A
A-10 Thunderbolt — 18
AV8B Harrier — 24

D
Dassault Mirage 2000 — 28
Dassault Rafale — 34

E
Eurofighter Typhoon — 40

F
F-2 Defense Fighter — 48
F-15 Eagle — 52
F-16 Fighting Falcon — 56
F-22 Raptor — 64
F-35 Joint Strike Fighter — 72
FA-18 Hornet — 80

M
MIG 29 — 86
MIG 31 — 90

P
Panavia Tornado — 94

S
SAAB Gripen — 98
Sukhoi SU-27 — 104
Sukhoi SU-35 — 108